Shapes of Time

Shapes of Time

GLENNA COOK

MoonPath Press

Copyright © 2022 Glenna Cook
All rights reserved.

No part of this publication may be reproduced, distributed, or transmitted in any form or by any means whatsoever without written permission from the publisher, except in the case of brief excerpts for critical reviews and articles. All inquiries should be addressed to MoonPath Press.

Poetry
ISBN 978-1-936657-65-0

Cover art: *Artemis*, charcoal, 29" x 22", from the 1990s series by the late Antja Kaiser, German born artist, longtime resident of Tacoma, Washington. Photographed and processed by Jim and Ginny Christensen

Author photo by Jim and Ginny Christensen

Book design by Tonya Namura, using Suave Script Pro, Avenir Next Condensed, and Minion Pro

MoonPath Press, an imprint of Concrete Wolf Poetry Series, is dedicated to publishing the finest poets living in the U.S. Pacific Northwest.

MoonPath Press
PO Box 445
Tillamook, OR 97141

MoonPathPress@gmail.com

http://MoonPathPress.com

*With love, for Ken,
my late husband of 63 years,
who supported me in so many ways*

Table of Contents

I. An Ordinary Day
New Year's Day, 5
An Ordinary Day, 6
A Poem Is, 7
The Clock, 8
Memories, 9
Pennsylvania Coal Town, 10
Discord, 11
Sanctuary, 12
Sleep, 13
Armchair Dreams, 14
Woodland Welfare, 15
Sparrow, 16
Too Close, 17
Necklace, 18
Tribe, 19
Worry, 20
Best Intentions, 21
How Morgan Sees Me, 22
A New Sound, 23
Desert Hermit, 24
October Wind, 25
All Things Must End, 26
Covid 19: The First Lockdown, 27
In and Out of Limbo, 28
Depression, 29
When things happen unexpectedly, 30
Sheltering in Place, 31
Thanksgiving, 32

II. Baptism
A Daughter's Story, 35
First Sunday School Lesson, 36
You Can't Fool God, 37
Cardamom, 38
Mrs. Spenser Has Curls Made of Iron, 39
Girls in Competition, 40
Monday, Washday, 41
Birthday, 42
At Ten I Discovered a New Kind of Beauty, 43
Baptism, 44
Two Grandmothers, 45
Accidental Cub Scout, 46
Bucking Logs, 47
Life Set to Explode, 48
In the Cool Breeze of a June Dawn, 49
A Daughter's Vigil, 51
Driving Down I-5, 53
Day of the Eclipse: August 21, 2017, 54
To My Son Upon His Father's Passing, 55
Writing a Letter to My Dead Husband
    While I Listen to Tchaikovsky's
    Capriccio Italian, 56
I dreamed you bought a car, 57
Widow's Song, 58
Christmas Eve 2020, 59
A Rose, 60

III. Shapes of Time
Memoir, 63
Could This Be Me?, 64
Moving Day, 65
New to the Neighborhood, 66
College Notes, 67

Smoking Weed with My Grandson, 69
Could We Not Learn from Them?, 70
Moonbeams, 71
Thanksgiving at the Grandchildren's Table, 72
Earth-Bound, 74
The Task, 76
In My Dream, I Looked and You Were Not There, 77
Hummingbirds in Winter, 78
Kin, 79
Country of Death, 81
End of Cycle, 82
Souvenir, 83
To Kafka from an Optimist, 84
The Other Side, 85
Discovery, 86
Ten Things to Do Before 10 AM, 87
Is There Such a Thing as Time?, 89
At Hazelwood Elementary, 91
Day of the Election Certification, 93
Hope's Flame, 94
Shapes of Time, 95
In Autumn, 96
When You Make an Apple Pie, 97

Acknowledgments, 99
Gratitude, 101
About the Author, 103

Shapes of Time

1. An Ordinary Day

New Year's Day

On a scarred oak table
sunrays illumine
three mandarin oranges
in a small blue bowl.
My resolution: pay attention.

An Ordinary Day

*It is out of the dailiness of life that one is driven into
the deepest recesses of the self.*
   —Stanley Kunitz

I wonder what caused Stanley to make this observation.

Was it the sun teasing in around his bedroom blind,
rousing him from deep sleep full of pleasant dreams?

Smell of coffee brewing, satisfaction
of its warm comfort as he read his morning paper?

Was it the walk he took with his dog after breakfast,
the talk with his neighbor over the fence?

Or the invitation from his yellow pad to write a poem,
the feel of the pen, the stream of words onto the page?

Gathering onions, garlic, and tomatoes
from his garden and chopping them for soup?

Quiet winding down as evening descended,
conversation with his wife, reading a good book?

Or was it that last moment before he lay himself
between cool sheets, his heart swelling with gratitude

for every simple gift of this ordinary day?

A Poem Is

A poem leads us through
cracks in our resistance.

Tall as a mountain—
fits into a teacup.
Deep as an ocean—
compressed as a pearl.

A poem can be a beggar
king, or ballerina.
Round as a stone,
jagged as a rock.

No fences or borders,
lots of open doors.
Goes where it wills,
says what it will,
strives to tell the truth.

It sometimes flies,
sometimes flows, sometimes
plods along a dusty road.

A poem is prose
dressed up for a party.

A poem is art.

The Clock

He bought it fifty years ago from a clock shop
long since out of business. At first

a source of pride, as years went by
he remembered less often to wind it.

Now that he's gone, I wind it every Wednesday, silence
it at night, hear its lusty gong throughout the day.

Its hand-crafted cherrywood case, shiny brass pendulum,
beveled glass door, remind me of a simpler time

that valued beauty over expedience.
Someday, I must get rid of such extravagance.

My kids say they have no room for it.
My grandkids want the speed of tech—

something small that thinks.
It keeps the hour and sings it out.

That's all it does.
That used to be enough.

Memories

At ninety-three, she lives in a retirement home
after husband of seventy years died.

It's been two years and she's still bitter and cold
that he didn't take her with him.

She wants to go, but her body,
still able to take her on daily walks, says no.

I have no purpose, she tells me.

Yes, I say, *you do. You have your memories.*

In the silence, her face softens.
She gazes at something far off.

I guess no one told her it is not a waste
of time, in her twilight years, to spin

the golden threads and weave them
into a garment that wraps her in comfort.

Pennsylvania Coal Town

after an Edward Hopper painting, 1947

He rakes the strip of bare ground
between lawn and foundation.
He thinks he might plant
lilacs. They would look good
against the yellow clapboard siding.

She would like them, he decides,
wondering why he didn't think
of this before. On the other side
of the window, she lies dying.
She may already be dead.
He doesn't want to know,
doesn't want to hear her last
breath, her sighs of forgiveness,
or see her reaching out to him.

He knows he didn't treat her right,
knows he took for granted her
devotion, let her work too hard
to please him. He didn't want
to be beholden, didn't
want her to see his empty heart
which kept him away too long
at the tavern most nights.

He wishes he could make it up
to her, somehow, but now he knows
it is too late, and he must
live without the memories
of good times together.

Discord

Neither wizard nor jester,
I cry tears for tomorrow's
sorrows. I'm a book written
up-side down.

You must stand on your head
to read me right-side up.

You congregate in your kitchens
holding knives and forks,
ready to eat each others' hearts,
living your lives in discord
rather than dance in a joyous circle.

Be aware. If love doesn't know
who you are, death will
introduce you. You will become
ghosts making love by the light
of the moon, unseen
in the absence of after-glow.

Sanctuary

It takes work not to worry
about what to do or not do,
how my actions might weigh

on the scales at the public
marketplace. It takes work
to separate myself

from the dull and sterile
Street of Expectations,
shoulder my way

through the crowd,
slip through a side
door into a quiet sanctuary,

set down all my unneeded
purchases and celebrate
my unencumbered self.

Sleep

You must treat sleep as a friend.
If it suspects you are in pursuit
or want more
than it is willing to give,
the battle is over.
It has fled.

You might as well get out of bed.

If you try to keep
your thoughts and worries
from its sight and wind them
into a tight ball,
it will spy the end
of the thread and pull,
leaving a tangled mess
on top of the hot covers.

It wants the upper hand,
won't be captured or cajoled.
It teases and taunts,
scampers just out of reach
and all this time
the clock is running.

Morning comes too soon,
chases it away.

Armchair Dreams

Every year, he buys a license, tunes
his motor, cleans his aluminum boat.

In his head, he holds a blueprint
of a room he'll add to the house.

Lumber waits in the garage. Every year,
his body grows weaker, more ridged with pain.

From the refuge of his recliner
he will build a room, he will

catch fish, his boat drifting
with the current on Commencement Bay.

Woodland Welfare

In the reddening of evening,
harlequin and duffle-head
ducks and a few coots
come in for a landing
on Lois Lake. A solitary
loon calls to her mate
from her nest.

Something prevents him
from coming to her aid—
a wildcat attack
perhaps, or an eagle.
The source of her sustenance
gives no response
to her desperate cry.

Does nature provide
for this kind of disaster?
What happens to the feathered
widow in the wild?

It is now dark
with a quarter moon above.
A mournful plea
pierces the calm
indifferent woods.

Sparrow

Out walking on a June afternoon,
I hear calls of distress
from a little brown sparrow
caught in the claws of a crow
pecking at it on the sidewalk.

Other crows sidle up,
eager for a share in the spoils.

A black cat streaks
into their circle,
grabs the bird
and takes off

up the bank and out of sight.

The disgruntled crows mill about
complaining among themselves.

The sparrow is silent.

Too Close

As I retrieve my morning paper in the frosty
pre-dawn, a large black lab watches me
from across the street. Light of the full moon

soon reveals two more dogs,
similar, but younger, sleek
as shadows, silent as my breath.

The three of then approach with purpose.
Bringing their cold hunger, they come too close.
I step inside and shut the door.

Necklace

An elephant died
for this necklace.

Bought in the marketplace
by a woman from America.

Made from a thick layer
of fat under the elephant's skin

which was cut into cubes, dried,
then turned on a lathe

into beads of various sizes.
The fat gives translucence.

Blood in the fat
glows a rosy color.

She paid little for it
but its value will increase

as the number of elephants
decreases.

Poachers killed it. They packed
its fat out of the jungle in pieces.

Tribe

We are the new homeless,
men and women, many with jobs,
some with children,
too many older than fifty,
living next to the curb in tents.
We multiply like cockroaches
while people in their houses
seek help to remove us
from their neighborhoods.

We spill out of our price-rising rentals,
packing what possessions we can
manage, find a settlement,
a gathering large enough to give
pause to those who want us gone.

Where else shall we go?

Two societies live side-by-side,
each unknown to the other.
Those housed survive by their privilege,
we, by our sheer numbers and skills
learned from the veterans of our tribe.

Worry

I hear a rat gnaw
within the wall of my bedroom.
How did it get in there?
Is there only one?
Will it make a hole?

I could be lying here in the dark
thinking about nuclear bombs
and two opposing leaders,
equally impetuous,
whose fingers are on their triggers.

Or global warming
that melts our ice caps,
raises the level of our seas,
causes ravenous wildfires,
and deadly hurricanes.

Instead, I can only think about
a rat gnawing in my wall.

Best Intentions

We worship the god of ourselves through our children,
project our dreams onto their dreams,
throw down our crowns, so they can be crowned.

The children bow under the burden
    of our longings.
They wish to eat fruit of our living.
They wish to drink milk of our joy.

They look into our eyes as into a mirror
    hoping to see happiness.
Instead, they see only striving.

We bow under the burden of our best intentions
while they need someone to teach them to dance.

How Morgan Sees Me

My two-year-old great-grandson
thinks he is king and I, his subject.

Surprisingly strong, he leads
me around the play yard by my finger,

shows me what he wants me to see,
speaks to me in a language

he expects me to understand.
I pretend I do, and obey his every

command, not wanting the slightest
frown to cloud his sweet imperial

countenance. Knowing he has this power
over me, he pushes it to the limit,

and I, completely besotted by this small
royal person, succumb to his will.

A New Sound

Keep silent, Grown-ups!
The children speak now.
Their voices rise
above our objections.

They are marching through,
an endless parade,
bearing signs, singing songs
spurred on by urgent need.

They witness us trashing
the planet we will leave
for their inheritance.
They ignore our empty
promises to save her,
our lame, piecemeal
solutions that cost us
almost nothing.

They cry out for sacrifice,
for clean and thoughtful
ways of living.

They have too much to lose
if they listen to us.

Keep silent
or sing their song.

Desert Hermit

He comes home from Afghanistan
in a tunnel of pain and depression,
longing for some kind of meaning
to fill his arid heart.

He tries a job or two,
then university. Finally,
the Arizona desert calls him,
lures him into its loneliness,
opens a new horizon
full of possibilities.

Away from the world's
attachments, he fills
his lungs with the dry
air that feels to him
like water to a salmon
that finds the stream
that brings it home.

October Wind

a sonnet

All shreds of summer flee before your bellow
that fans the leaves to brilliant fire.
Uninvited, overbearing fellow,
you upset the complaisance I desire.
You crash into my mellow season,
toss everything unfastened in your path.
Even the tall firs shudder, and with reason.
The shallow-rooted topple in your wrath.

Then, you leave, and the quiet gloom
of shortened days, sodden and dreary,
lack your vigor. Before the promised bloom
of new life, I grow pale and weary.
So, rude and lusty friend, I fondly greet
your growl, your rough kiss on my cheek.

All Things Must End

These last golden rays of September
will give way to darker,
colder, more turbulent skies.

Every season holds
hints of the final season.
Each new beginning dawns
more tenuously.
Each year finds me more alone,
left behind to live
with ghostly memories
of those I loved.

Time slows; a quiet lethargy descends.
The incoming tide grows slack,
gives in to the moon's persistent pull.
Should I give in
or resist the undertow?

In the still-dark hours of morning
I push myself out of bed,
swallow a battery of pills,
eat a healthy breakfast,
and drive to the gym to pedal.

Covid 19: The First Lockdown

My calendar looks empty as my day.
All the places I could go closed down.
I yearn to visit my family.

Meanwhile, skies clear,
waterways look cleaner,
wildlife takes a calm breath.

In the park, the grass has not been cut
for weeks. Tiny white daisies
and golden dandelions flourish.

Until they told me I must stay
within this shell of my house,
I didn't know how strong as steel
my need to gather.

My calendar looks empty as my day.
All the places I could go, closed down.
I yearn to visit my family.

In and Out of Limbo

*. . . but while everybody was asleep, an enemy came and
sowed weeds among the wheat, and then went away.*
    —Matthew 13:25, NRSV Bible

As Covid 19 drags into the ninth month,
my heart aches for the world's pain.
My throat constricts around words of hope,
my feet stick to the ground, my hands
hang useless from idle arms.

A conniving devil roams the land, sowing
weeds of deception and dissent among the wheat.
Though it's tempting to listen to news of his gleeful
mischief-making lies, I decide

he's caught enough of my attention.
While listening to a Bach concerto
on the radio, I eat granola
topped with sliced peach
ripened to perfection, and sip
my morning coffee, savoring its warm
bitterness, its welcome jolt of energy.

The September sun promises a glorious day.

I take a walk around my neighborhood,
greet flowers in peoples' yards
and think of all I cherish: friends and family
my house, my town, the Yorkshire terrier
who barks when I pass by her fence.

Depression

A thick gray blanket
wraps me, holds me inside
its soft cocoon.

I know I must struggle
against its seduction,
connect with the outside world.

Inwardness can be good,
can make one wise.
Not within the gray blanket.

Inwardness must be able
to breath in and breathe out.
This blanket suffocates.

When things happen unexpectedly,

a dark wind blowing me off-course
without a compass or words spoken
from an unknown source to guide me.

If I forget to be scared,
I'll look within and follow
my North Star through uncharted
waters to a new destination.

I can't always stroll in an orchard
of bliss. To live a rich life, I must
stretch toward the unease
of uncertainties never explored.

That tarantula walking
across my path might be a threat
or an opportunity to face
an unfounded fear.

Sheltering in Place

Inside this house, a quiet peace,
outside, strident voices, silent peril.

My inclination grows
to keep the outside out.

I turn the TV off,
turn the radio to music.

Social media draws me in
until I tire of its chatter.

Though my grandfather clock ticks
and gongs, time inside my house

stops, a repetition of music and books,
writing and phone calls and on-line

conversations. People speak to me from little
boxes on a screen, outside coming in.

While I sit in my house, an angry outside
drama of social distance and masks plays on.

Eventually, I know,
outside and inside again must meet.

What will the world be like?
I hear rumors and want to stay inside.

Your letters comfort me.
They speak of new birth,

celebration, remembrance
of a time we knew.

Thanksgiving

Thanks for the brief glimpse
of a car's front fender in my mirror
just before changing lanes
on the freeway this morning.

Thanks for my mix-up of time
so I arrived at the art fair at closing
and made a new artist friend
as I helped her repack her paintings.

Thanks for Parkinson's Disease
that has taught me to cherish life,
live it well, and accept
that which I can't control.

Thanks for the only available
independent-living apartment
in the senior facility complex
which perfectly fits my needs.

Thanks for those sixty-three years
spent with my difficult man that I loved,
who tempered me to withstand
this present time of turmoil.

Thanks for my childhood
as a lonely, misfit girl
who lived in a world of books
and turned into a poet.

II. *Baptism*

A Daughter's Story

She cried over news of my coming.
I spoiled her plans.

At my birth, she tried to cuddle me.
I made my back stiff.

She tried to read to me.
I slipped off her lap.

She tried to mold me into a dancing princess.
I turned out a leaping frog.

She tried to find me in a flower garden.
I stayed hidden among the trees.

In her last years, she needed me.
I was there at her side.

First Sunday School Lesson

Two pictures hang
on my Sunday school wall.
One I know is Jesus.
The other must be God.

Jesus is smiling at children.
God looks rather stern.
He is Jesus' father.
That's all I know about him.

You Can't Fool God

Four years old, I walk
to Sunday School with my brother.

In my hand I hold
two pennies.

Walking home, I tell him
I put only one in the basket.

God will know,
he says.

I don't care.
I want to buy candy.

At the little store
one block from home

no one stands behind the counter.
The door is locked.

I'm slumped on the steps
when Brother comes to get me.

It closes on Sunday,
he tells me, and leads me home.

Cardamom

It's almost Easter and a memory rises
like the yeast in Mrs. Anderson's
sweet rolls. She made them every
Saturday morning for her four
grown children and their spouses
crowded into her kitchen
for coffee and conversation.

I lived across the street, knew
just when to come, and sat
with them, a quiet little mouse,
nibbling on the warm sweetness.

Mrs. Anderson was Finnish
and said *tink* instead of *think*,
dis, instead of *this*.

The day before Easter, she made
hot-crossed buns. When I asked her
what made her kitchen smell
so good, she whispered,
with a smile and a wink,
her well-guarded secret.

Mrs. Spenser Has Curls Made of Iron

Mrs. Spenser sits at the back of the class.

Mrs. Spenser speaks only when teaching.

Mrs. Spenser has a ruler for slapping hands.

Mrs. Spenser lives with witches.

Mrs. Spenser lives in an icehouse.

Mrs. Spenser likes only smart kids.

Mrs. Spenser turns dumb kids into sheep.

Mrs. Spenser turns unruly kids into stone.

Mrs. Spenser can make you disappear.

Mrs. Spenser has a weakness.

Mrs. Spenser can't hurt you if you disappear.

Girls in Competition

My brothers taught me
to cherish a good fight, and Eileen,
teal-blue eyes deep as canyons,
cute button nose in a field of freckles,
provided the perfect rival.

Whether hopscotch, baseball,
track, or a spelling bee,
we went at it with gusto,
our endurance tested
as much as our skills.

I know I've had more successes in life
because of that snippy little redhead
bombshell who gave me no rest
from third grade through high school.
Though I've not seen her
for thirty-five years,
she still hounds me.

Monday, Washday

When I come home from school,
acrid wood smoke hangs heavy
in the cold persistent drizzle.

I enter the dense heat of the living room
filled with racks of wet laundry. One sits atop
the heating stove, drying father's work clothes.

It's Monday, and Mother has saved
the socks and handkerchiefs for me to hang
on the wooden rods, then put away as they dry.

Birthday

It happened just that once
on my seventh birthday.

It didn't last—just
that one blissful moment

when I looked back to see
myself at six, and then

stepped forward
a different me—

a taller, smarter version
of whom I had been.

I knew I was loved.
Of course, I was loved

but I so wanted them to see
this amazing girl I had become.

I wanted them to tell me
I was perfect.

At Ten I Discovered
a New Kind of Beauty

It grew among the weeds
between the two bare
rocky tire tracks of the driveway.
Only one, and like no other

I had seen. A small flower,
apricot-colored petals
fringed around
an apricot daisy eye.

I stood for a long time
in the spell of it,
raised in my hand against
the August blue sky

and wondered
why those two pure colors
next to each other
filled me with such awe.

Baptism

As a child of twelve,
immersed three times
in the pool's cool water,
I emerge from each name
of the Father,
Son, and Holy Ghost
gasping for breath,
uncomprehending.

After Mother and my aunt
help me out of my dripping
clothes and into my new Easter
dress, a strange light claims me,
names me,
nestles in my solar plexus,

a mystery never solved.

Two Grandmothers

One grandmother,
I was too young to remember,
the other died before my birth,
so I conjured them in my mind
to make up for their absence.

Each gave me a gift from the other
side, one, a pen with feathers that can
write in all colors, the other,
a perspective from which I can see
the world in a way no one can but me.

A world refracted with brilliance,
like spring, blossoming in shining
light, or fractured into darkness,
like winter, shadowing my life
with secrets for me to uncover.

Those gifts of fate my grandmothers
gave me are woven into my destiny—
threads of possibility, threads of struggle—
in a design unique to me, even as I move
someday, to the other side.

Accidental Cub Scout

With the boys in my mother's cub scout den,
I was allowed to unravel the edges of a square-yard
of fabric for a tablecloth for Mother's Day, watched
a potter turn a lump of clay into a vase and learned from
a woodcarver how to carve a wooden chain. But I wasn't
allowed to use a knife, or make a kite to fly in a contest,
or play football after den meetings.

When the boys cleared a spot in our woods
for a sleep-over, I pitched in with zeal, imagining
the bliss of sleeping under the stars, but I was told,
No girls allowed!

That night, they got into a fir-cone fight. One
boy got a bloody nose, and my parents got in trouble
from his parents for not keeping a closer eye. It served
them right. I should've been there.

Bucking Logs

The saw whispers back and forth
through the trunk of a fir tree
felled in our woods by the wind.
My brother's youthful arms work
one end of the six-foot bucksaw
in rhythm with Dad's
stronger push and pull.

The day is warm.
Green-dappled sunlight filters
through a canopy of leaves.
Bees nuzzle red blossoms
of a wild currant bush.

Now and then, the saw sticks.
Dad waits for Brother
to sprinkle oil on the blade.
Sometimes Dad pounds
a wedge with a sledge-
hammer to widen the cut.

Sweat shines their faces,
their tanned and shirtless torsos.
Neither speaks
except to the task, nor notices me,
little sister
sitting with my back
against a maple tree.

Life Set to Explode

They came in a bag of hand-me-downs
from Mother's friend's daughter.
Mother would never have let me buy them.

They rounded my rump deliciously,
set off my legs with a flair.

Boys came around
who ignored me before,
one roaring up on his Harley.

In those red corduroy shorts
I knew I was dynamite.

In the Cool Breeze of a June Dawn

Morning after high school graduation.
Only five a.m. and I can't sleep.
My wedding in two weeks.

I throw off my covers, dress,
slip past him, asleep
on our couch, and escape
into the cool breeze of a June dawn.

I follow the creek down to the pond
where chickadees chirp a lively
chorus and hummingbirds sip
from thimble berry blossoms.
Dragon flies perform their mating
dance above the still water.

I should feel happy.
My future looks good.
I love the man I'm to marry.
Then why do I feel loss?

Last night at the reception,
I moved down the line of teachers,
shaking their hands. I didn't think
I felt one way or another
about not seeing them again.

Halfway down the line
I began to cry.
Not gentle tears, either.
Tears out of control,
an ocean at high tide
from deep within,
and they wouldn't stop.

How embarrassing!
My parents and husband-to-be
didn't know what to do with me.

So, here I am, a girl of eighteen,
soon to be a bride,
sheltered in my favorite
place of solitude, my refuge
when I'm feeling melancholy,
and I wonder
how much of me must I give up?

A Daughter's Vigil

1.
Mother is dying,
her time honed
to an edge of days.

When I am with her,
death wraps us gently
in its soft presence.
When I go away,
it follows me out the door
into my hum-drum existence.

Mother is dying.
How will I dispose of her things?

2.
Patience.
She is dying
slowly,

has lived
a full, rich life.

I hold her hand,
happy when her eyes
open and she smiles
to see me here.

I don't wish
her meager life to linger.
Nor do I wish her to leave.

Patience.
Wait, while she dreams

and drifts
away on a slow,
slow
stream.

Driving Down I-5

In pewter mid-day light
we speed past turgid rivers.
Soaked cows graze in soggy pastures.

Slap of rain on windshield,
snick, snick of wipers,
tires' watery rasps
fill the silence between us.

Even the words we might speak
are dampened.

Day of the Eclipse: August 21, 2017

Even as the sun shrank to the thinnest sliver
the loss of light was undramatic.

Now, in the aftermath, as my afternoon tea steeps,
I stand looking out at the sunny day.

I'll wait for stories from those who traveled
miles to see the moon conquer the whole

and the earth respond in awestruck darkness.
I chose, instead, to stay home with my husband.

Unfazed by it all, he sits in his recliner
tapping keys of his laptop.

I wonder, again, if he is lonely
when I'm not here, the house quiet, as it is now.

Guilt sends me with my tea
into the living room to keep him company.

Deep into research of something,
he ignores me. I smile

toward the comfort of my own room
where I write about eclipses.

To My Son Upon His Father's Passing

How is your belt?
were the last words
he said to you
or to anyone
before he slipped into that dream
from which he never awoke.

We knew he meant
How is your back?
and that his very last word,
though it came out wrong,
was caring.

Do you remember those words,
or only the ones he didn't speak,
or those he spoke that hurt?

No one taught him, in his neglected
childhood, the right words to express
as a father, yet I know he loved you
because he told me.

He wanted you to love him too,
and for your sake, someday
I hope you will.

Writing a Letter to My Dead Husband
While I Listen to Tchaikovsky's *Capriccio Italian*

My heart is a herd
of wild horses
galloping
galloping
across the plain

while the rain comes down
the rain
the rain comes down

Wild horses gallop
across the plain
while the rain comes down

the rain

I dreamed you bought a car

against my knowledge and wishes.
A big, gas-guzzling, luxury monster.

I made up my mind not to forgive you
even though, in all our years of marriage,

I always did. Yet
how can I stay angry?

It was only a dream and only a car,
and you, my love, are gone.

Widow's Song

a villanelle

Why am I here and you are gone?
Did you think I wouldn't mind?
I sing each day a lonely song.

Why couldn't you take me along?
To leave me alone was so unkind.
Why am I here and you are gone?

Much in this messed up world seems wrong.
It can't hurt you, but I'm left behind
to sing each day a lonely song.

The years I wait stretch, oh, so long
I seem to lose all track of time.
Why am I here and you are gone?

The older I get, the less I belong
and lighter to this world I bind.
I sing each day a lonely song.

Until I go, I'll live among
those whom I love and who remind
me why I'm here while you are gone.
They'll sing with me a less lonely song.

Christmas Eve 2020

Family once filled this living room
on Christmas Eve, where now I sit alone.

When the gang burst through the front door,
what a commotion they made
as they greeted one another with hugs,
piled gifts around the tree,
set down food and drink where room
could be found on countertop or table.

The silence in this house tonight
sounds louder than their noisy voices.

This year, Covid 19 dictates we keep
distance between us, wear masks,
mingle outside or stay home
in self-imposed quarantine. Tomorrow,

I'll call on family members to share
gifts and air-hugs outside their doors.
For dinner, I'll join my son's family
around propane heaters on their deck.
We will all try to hold onto some part

of the Christmas we remember,
while yearning for next year, when
we can gather without wearing masks,
give each other hugs that aren't just arms
reaching out into cold empty air.

A Rose

An array of flowers
confronts my senses
as I walk into Fred Meyer's.

At checkout, a young man behind me
places a bouquet of red
roses on the counter.

Someone is going to be happy,
I say.

His eyes light up and he smiles.

In the parking lot
he steps beside my cart,
sticks a long-stemmed rose
into my bag and whispers,
Happy Valentine's Day,
then walks away.

My startled, *Thank you,*
trails behind him.

He can't have known
this is my first Valentine's Day
in sixty-three years
without *my* Valentine.

And, *oh!* I hadn't known
how much I needed this rose,
its regal red head rising proudly
out of the brown paper bag.

III. *Shapes of Time*

Memoir

Shards of broken glass
strew the path behind me—
rainbow-colored splinters
of spent days.

If I tell my story
most will be lies—fertile
soil where blood-red tulips
grow or dust the wind
blows where it will.

Memory, jesting trickster,
constructs what it wants
me to believe.

I'll retrieve some colored
pieces and cobble together
a lively tale, hoping
someone wants to hear.

Truth may begin there
among the fused shards.

Could This Be Me?

after Charles Simic

i.
Silent wind
sailing over the sea
without a whoosh without
breaking the sound barrier

ii.
A chicken
sitting on her nest
clucking in alarm
over a broken egg

iii.
A sparrow
with a broken wing
appealing for help
from a silent crow

iv.
A guitar
with a broken string
and a sad heart
wishing it were a saxophone

Moving Day

The rocking of the boat
sailing me away from home
brings forth a churning in my gut.

I shove aside the backward
yearning for the familiar
happiness I leave behind.

I will be a guest in a foreign
country, learning a new
language, thrust into stunned
silence in the ceremony

of new beginnings. The moon looks
down with empathy, and sighs.
It will be like a birthday
the candles unlit with fire.

New to the Neighborhood

After an afternoon nap on the couch
and a cup of peppermint tea,
I go outside to take a walk.

The bright October sun pulls
the neighbors out of their houses.
They smile at me as they pass.

I'm new to the neighborhood, so
know nothing about their lives.
Their faces remind me of new

moons, dark with potential for knowing,
or blank slates I can write on
without expectation or judgment.

I kick at the maple leaves strewn
on my path. Over-ripe fruit rots
beneath a persimmon tree, giving

off an odor of treacle.
From a stroller, a baby's laugh floats
into the crisp air, sweet as birdsong.

College Notes

Age fifty-eight, still married,
kids flown, early retirement,
I graduate from college.

Now, years later
clearing clutter from my past,
I find this box of classroom notes.
Did I suppose I would someday
read them? Recover kernels
of knowledge from the mass
that has slipped away?
I could gather what I retained,
put it into a hazelnut shell
with plenty of room to spare.

Yet, it changed me.
I learned the inner world of plants.
Like us, their gametes meet
to carry on their species.
I learned that Earth, a living body
always in a swirl of motion—
coughing up, pressing down,
wrinkling and gouging—
floats on her plates wherever it suits her,
though we don't see it,
our lives a flicker to her eons.

I saw how wave after wave of civilizations
cresting high on lust for power, crashed
on rocky shores of hubris.
The pulling tide of humanity
swept them all into a common sea.

I learned to love irony and be a skeptic,
that East leans more right-brained than West,
that it's been a man's world far too long,
how to say in French,
C'est la vie. J'aime la vie.

That's life. I love life.

Smoking Weed with My Grandson

We're overlooking Chiricahua
Monument, a sacred place
for those who came before.
In the canyon below,
stone formations look like people.

My grandson needs a joint to ease
pain in his messed-up neck.
Result of an IED blast.
Souvenir from Afghanistan.

He sees me watching and offers me a drag.
I've never smoked pot, but I accept.
He seems surprised and a little amused.

We stand side-by-side
silently passing the joint
back and forth,
taking in the breathtaking view.
I pull three big puffs
but I must have done something wrong
because, when he asks me, *Do you feel it?*
I say, *Not really.*

How do I get high on pot
when I'm already high on happiness?

Could We Not Learn from Them?

      Consider the lowly virus,
each entity nothing in itself
but working together
a vicious army.

      Intelligent
beyond our grasp, they know
all about us, of our need to mingle,
going out when we could stay at home
not exposing others.

      They know
where we are weakest and attack
our sensitive membranes to pass
themselves along through our sneezes,
coughs, and couplings.

      Masters of adaptation,
they mutate to slip by
our latest defenses, change keys
as we invent new locks. They survive
by learning from their defeats.

Moonbeams

to my great-granddaughter, Madeline

Don't wish for the moon, Maddie.
It's out of reach.
No matter what they tell you

you'll never own the moon. Wish
for moonbeams to light your path,
lunar reflection on a calm sea,
friendly wink of a thin, golden crescent.

Wish for waking in the morning to birdsong,
smooth sand under your feet on the beach,
a friend you can trust to keep your secrets,

a maple tree's shade on a hot afternoon,
sweet tartness of lemonade.

Thanksgiving at the Grandchildren's Table

One place left at the grandchildren's table
and I take it. They welcome me
and say I'm young at heart.
I'm eighty-one.

No longer babies,
these kids have jobs:
pipefitter, electrician,
teacher, mail-carrier,
molecular biologist.

The mail carrier, who also paints,
tells me his recent paintings are dark.
I say we live in dark times.
The pipefitter says,
statistically speaking,
things are better than they've ever been.

He passes the butter and tells me
to stop listening to gloomy news
that fear-mongers spread.
They all agree.

I want to believe them,
to enter into their optimistic,
carefree view of the world.

I thought my task as grandmother
was to pass along the wisdom
I've learned through years of living.
I was wrong.

The teacher pours me a glass
of sour beer, the latest trend.
I join them in their light-hearted
talk and laughter.
At the grandchildren's table,
for an hour, I feel young.

Earth-Bound

Not all two-year-olds can jimmy the lock
intended to keep them from escaping
the safety of their house and venturing
into the concrete perils of the world.

Morgan can.

No matter the child-safety device—
chain, or turned knob, or wooden
chair jammed under the doorknob—
he masters them all, and there is nothing
wishy-washy about his resolve

to flee out
the kitchen door,
head down the long,
rocky driveway
to the road,
where cars speed
around the curve,
ignoring the flashing
yellow sign
that reads,
Slow Down.

A child's soft flesh is no match for the hard
body of a car, and his imagination
knows no difference between its earth-bound
weight and the lightness of a wind-blown cloud.

The car brakes in time, and his anguished
mother trembles in relief.

Her delighted son
laughs with glee to see
he has the power to make it stop.

The Task

I remember one day, as a child
I refused to make my bed,
dawdling for over an hour, while
I yearned to be outside
in the warm sunshine and the sweet
fragrance of the summer day.

I heard my mother's repeated scolds
from the other side of the door
until she finally burst in like
a windstorm and gave me a spanking,
like I knew she eventually would.

Crying from the injustice of it all,
it took me two minutes to make the bed.

Don't we make our own weather?
I'm 86 now, and whenever I try to evade
a task, even one with its own rewards,
my mother, with her rough
gritty edges, and dead for 22 years,
still hovers over me like a kingfisher
over an elusive fish.

In My Dream, I Looked and You Were Not There

We were walking down a country road,
when you crossed without me to the other side.

Did the thick woods swallow you?
I look among the hungry alders.

If only you would tell me
why you left.

If only you would tell me
if you are coming home.

Are you all right?
Will I see you again?

I am so alone looking for you,
who may not want to be found.

Hummingbirds in Winter

On my apartment balcony
at least a dozen hummingbirds
horde around the bird feeder.
Their frantic activity jars
my impression of exotic isolates
sipping daintily from
throats of garden blossoms.

These greedy little guzzlers, common
as robins, fight among themselves
for their turn at the trough.

Among the species, only Annas
winter over, and in this snowy
December, I understand their
desperate need for nourishment.

I grow dizzy from watching
their acrobatic maneuvers,
swift dives and ascensions,
twists and turns, hovering,
then dashing off at bullet-speed.
I try to make sense of their
movements as they change
places in a nano-second.

One could never make friends
with a hummingbird.

Kin

A friend of mine,
one cold and windy
March morning, paused
on his front porch
to notice a bumble bee,
motionless, on the railing.
A quiver of antennae
told him it lived.

Moved to pity, he warmed
a shot glass and turned
it over the bee. For a while,

the bee stayed still, then slowly
began to crawl, until
it reached a glass
wall. My friend
slid the tiny greenhouse
along with the bee's progress.

Sunrays warmed the air
within and, in time,
my friend raised
the glass and the bee
flew out
into the buffeting
wind.

In a world
where millions of creatures
big and small,
even whole species

disappear every year,
it may not seem like much
to save one such little insect.

As my friend's story ended,
we shared a kinship
with this endangered
bumble bee and hoped
for its survival.

Country of Death

I am not ready to sit at the bedside
of our beautiful planet, Earth.

I walk quietly, reverently, upon her grass,
breathe in her sacred air that we pollute,

look out at her life-giving sea
that we poison with our plastic.

I weep for her madness, caused by toxins
found even in her rain.

I, too, am dying, but of old age,
going the way of the planet, but at a natural pace.

Soon we may both be in the country of death.
Soon, we may all be in the country of death.

End of Cycle

When it grows old
the trillium turns
from white to purple

Last light of day
bruise on your hand
eyelids weeping

Souvenir

A tiny wine glass, probably not meant
for wine at all, but something stronger.
Not crystal-clear, a slight brownish
tint, cut with fine design. I sorted it out
to bring with me when I moved
to Bradley Park senior community.

A singular item, one of my favorite things.
I sometimes brought it to dinner in the dining
room, along with a little jar of wine.

My Uncle George brought it back with him
from Germany, after World War II,
I would say to my table
companions when they asked.

Last night I broke it.

I set it on the table, empty, inside its sack
to bring home, and it tipped over.
The women at my table acted more
heartbroken than I at its destruction.
Loss after loss has taught me
to accept and let go what is gone.

It's only a piece of glass, I said,
knowing another piece of me had just died.

To Kafka from an Optimist

*I have the true feeling of myself only when
I am unbearably unhappy.*
    —*Franz Kafka*

If I am doomed and heaven
is a lie, why should you care
that I refuse to travel down
your dark corridors of despair?

If there is no God,
can it be sin if I should choose
to keep imagining a higher being
who cares for me? What can I lose?

When you see only darkness
and I see light at dawn,
am I a fool to live as if there's hope
when there is none?

If this is all there is, if only a black
void will meet me at my end
and I find it was all for nothing,
will it really have been?

The Other Side

The other side of anticipation
    is worry.

The other side of orange
    is ocean blue.

The other side of elation is shyness
    and confusion.

The other side of bird song
    is whale song.

The other side of stillness is a pebble
    tossed into a pond.

The other side of white is ominous gray
    startled by zebra stripes of lightning.

The other side of joy is a siren
    wailing in darkness.

The other side of grief
    is gratitude.

Discovery

God, why did you give me two childhoods:
one full of bliss, the other
painful to remember?

Why did you give this odd and rowdy girl
a frame too small to contain
its wild extremities?

Was it you who told my elders to control
my strong and willful spirit? My
voice pitched too free

for their courteous ears, turned into silent
daydreams, my careless joy
ceded to compliance.

And now, I discover it was you, God, who placed
within me that unquenchable spark
which made me shake

my raging fist at you and turn away, and you who
followed me through the far country
of my prideful blundering.

Now, I am sore from falling on your stumbling
stone. Now, I know you love my
stubborn striving ways,

my strong and willful spirit—my voice.
Only now do I believe I can
never disappoint you.

Ten Things to Do Before 10 AM

according to my healthcare insurance
provider, from an e-mail received
on my 84th birthday

1) Get up as soon as you wake up.
   It's my birthday!

2) Make your bed.
   What, you're my mother?

3) Breathe deep.
   I'm eighty-four.

4) Pour juice of a lemon into a glass of water
   and drink.
   Seriously?

5) Fuel up with a good breakfast of fat, protein,
   and carbohydrates.
   Bagel with lox and cream cheese.

6) Move around.
   Or not.

7) Write three pages in longhand.
   Write big.

8) Connect your heart: call or text a person
   (who hasn't passed)
   or send a snail-mail.

9) Do one task that's hard or unpleasant.
   Clean out the litter box.

10) Do something fun.
   Write a poem.

Is There Such a Thing as Time?

I'm late! I'm late!
How can I be late if there is no time?
No time is walking
down numberless streets,
a mist blocking the future, the past
a question of the reality
of dreams. If I am to be
at a certain place at a certain
time and there is no time,
how can I be late?

Even a beetle, who has no sense
of time, is worthy
of the earth's protection.
If there is no time how can I be worthy
or unworthy? How can
I be late?

Let's hypothesize for a moment
a proposal of my present self.

I wake up in the morning
with a multitude of choices.
How will I spend my time?
Do I carry within myself a divine
intention which I am supposed
to discern and follow
toward an unknown
purpose, a willed action
which is only mine to fulfill?
What if I miss the mark,
make the wrong choice,
blindly choose
the wrong path?

Every day, someone's
young nephew gets on
his bicycle and pedals
out of time, still believing
in the reality of dreams,
riding toward a peaceful
future of willed action.

At Hazelwood Elementary

for Melissa

A boy sits beside his third-grade teacher
fifteen minutes before lunch break ends.
He wears an air of cockiness in the way
he holds his shoulders and in the wary
defiance in his brown eyes,
almost hidden by dark bangs.

He used to be trouble, using his loud
voice to disrupt the lessons, leading
his ring of followers to do the same.
He liked to see his teacher
try not to be angry.

She's young and pretty, skilled
in her craft, yet still vulnerable
as a rose without its thorns.

At the end of her patience,
she invites him to the classroom
during lunch break, to talk.
He thinks, *no*,
but comes anyway
and finds her knitting.

He's not sure what to say.
She knits, he talks.
He talks, she listens.
He tells her what he can't
tell anyone else.
His parents fight,

he can never please his dad,
how hard it is to sit still in class,
and when his dog died, he cried.

Day by day, he comes
fifteen minutes before lunch break ends.
He talks, she listens
and knits.

Day of the Election Certification

January 6, 2021

I have sat for hours
eyes glued to the TV,
watching a murderous mob
storm our nation's Capital.

I rise from my chair
as if from a bad dream,
stretch tense muscles and look
out my window. The late
afternoon sun hovers
above the horizon. Suddenly

fast as a gazelle, something
streaks past and out of sight.
Soon it comes back, slower now,
adjusting a slipped headpiece.

It's Olive, my four-year-old
neighbor, dressed as an alligator
and here comes two-year-old
Mosby, in costume as a bee,
bumbling along the sidewalk
beside his father.

It's January, *not* Halloween,
but they don't care. For them
every day is a day to celebrate.

Hope's Flame

Flickering in the night's raging tempest
tended by brave souls
who guard it with their bodies,
a flame, true and beautiful,
struggles to endure.

By its nature it survives
not from privilege or might
but from love's humble acts
of sacrifice and service.

Endangered as it always seems
of being extinguished,
it has burned through the ages.

I place my trust
in this ancient beacon
rather than the cruel wind
ever threatening to quench it.

Shapes of Time

I used to think my ankles
were the best-looking part of me—
slim as flower stems, with a classy knob
of bling sporting each side. Now
at certain times, say, a hot day in August,
they resemble two Bratwurst sausages.

My once graceful hands, fingers
slender and nimble, performed
with ease every task I assigned.
Now, enlarged bony knuckles trap
rings, have trouble with buttons,
and can't open a jar.

My dainty rose-petal ears
could hear the softest whisper.
Now, grown like cabbages,
they no longer decipher lyrics of songs.

My heart, I'm happy to say,
with tough, bitter endurance,
weathered the times and improved with age.
It's etched by scars of grief, thickened
to protect, and so loosely assembled
that love seeps out through every seam.

In Autumn

In my eighties I've entered autumn,
time of harvest, time of loss,
my body a dry leaf hanging onto a tree branch.

I see myself diminish, my height
having shrunk three inches. Most of my teeth wear
crowns, scars throughout my body mark
where defective parts are missing. My hair has
lost its color, my eyes their sharp vision,
my skin its smooth tautness.

The light slowly changes from summer's glare
to a golden glow deepening into twilight.
It's time to contemplate, recover
my scattered pieces, tend my wounds, cast
off past regrets, anxieties about the future.

In a frantic world full of sorrow and strife,
I have earned the right
to be still, to drift at a leisurely pace and
appear to be wise.

When You Make an Apple Pie

You think you have enough room
for four apples, but you don't, so you use
three and save the other for lunch.

After you have laid down
the top crust, poked air holes
in the shape of an "A," pinched
together top and bottom,
there's always an excess
around the edges, which you cut away.

You don't toss it out.
You roll it, spread with butter,
sprinkle with cinnamon and sugar,
bake for twelve minutes,
then eat with your afternoon tea.

I know when I die
I will leave behind a long
list of books I wanted to read,
friends I could have shared
pie and coffee with more often,
trips I could have taken,
poems I could have written.

In the end
it will all be enough.

Acknowledgments

The poet thanks the following publications in which her poems appeared, sometimes in previous versions.

Puget Sound Poetry Connections Anthologies

Ariel: "Could We Not Learn from Them?"

Limbo or Liminal: "Christmas Eve 2020"

Windblown: "To Kafka from an Optimist," "Tribe," "A Daughter's Story"

Gratitude

My heartfelt gratitude to:

Lana Hechtman Ayers for her faith in me and for expert editing;

Amy Whitcomb for her helpful initial editing;

Debra Wöhrmann and Kay Mullen for reading my work and giving excellent suggestions and support;

Josie Turner and Michael Magee for reading my manuscript and giving their impressions for the back cover;

Connie K Walle for keeping a culture of poetry alive in Tacoma for three decades as president of Puget Sound Poetry Connection;

all my good friends in PSPC, past and present, who, over the years have provided a home-base for my poetry;

all the members of my Poetry Play group, which meets every Thursday and keeps my poetry juices flowing;

the people of Immanuel Presbyterian Church, who have been my most enthusiastic cheerleaders;

and for all my friends and family, who have been loving supporters, and sometimes, even interesting subjects to write about.

About the Author

This is Glenna Cook's second full-length collection of poems. The first, *Thresholds*, was published by MoonPath Press in 2017, and was a finalist for the Washington State Book Award for Poetry in 2018.

Cook grew up in Olympia, Washington, where, at age 18, she married her husband, Kenneth. They had 3 children (their oldest, a son, died of cancer in 2016 at age 60), and have 9 grandchildren and 8 great-grandchildren. After a 25-year career with the telephone company, she retired from U.S. West Communications in 1990, then immediately enrolled in college. She graduated from the University of Puget Sound Magna cum Laude in 1994 at age 58 with a BA in English Literature. While at university, she won the Hearst Essay Prize for the Humanities and the Nixeon Civille Handy Prize in poetry. She is a Hedgebrook alumna and a member of Phi Kappa Phi.

She has read her poetry many places in the Puget Sound region, and published dozens of poems in journals and anthologies, such as *Raven Chronicles, Spindrift, crosscurrent review, Trillium,* and *Kind of a Hurricane Anthologies.*

Her husband died in 2018, after 63 years of marriage. Cook has Parkinson's disease, which she keeps at bay with medicine, diet, and a rigorous exercise program. She serves as an advocate for others with Parkinson's disease. She loves reading, watching Masterpiece Theater and Netflix on TV, taking walks, and interacting with people. Two of her favorite sayings are: *We make our own weather*, and (from Rumi) *What you seek is seeking you.*

www.ingramcontent.com/pod-product-compliance
Lightning Source LLC
Chambersburg PA
CBHW030156100526
44592CB00009B/312